big cakes

WTHE AUSTRALIAN **Women's Weekly**

contents

chocolate cakes   4

layered cakes   22

feather-light cakes   40

celebration cakes   58

glossary   74

conversion chart   77

index   78

Cakes are my absolute favourite thing to bake; I'll make at least one cake every weekend, much to the delight of my family and friends. With cake baking it's all about experience, so keep practising. Be careful when weighing and measuring your ingredients and follow the recipe using the mixing, baking and cooling advice.

Pamela Clark

Editorial & Food Director

Australian cup and spoon measurements are metric. A conversion chart appears on page 77.

chocolate cakes

What's not to love about a delicious and decadent chocolate cake? From a date & chocolate torte to a hazelnut mud, this chapter has something for even the most die-hard chocoholics.

tips It's important to measure the closed springform pan; the measurement that appears on the base of the springform pan sometimes refers to the size of the pan when it is open. This rich flourless cake can be made with other dried fruit, such as figs, or a combination of raisins, currants and sultanas, and with an orange liqueur instead of brandy.

chocolate, prune & almond fudge cake

- 1¼ cups (210g) seeded prunes, chopped
- ⅔ cup (160ml) brandy
- 165g (5 ounces) dark eating (semi-sweet) chocolate, chopped
- 165g (5 ounces) butter, chopped
- ¾ cup (165g) caster (superfine) sugar
- 4 eggs
- 2 cups (240g) ground almonds

1 Preheat oven to 160°C/325°F. Grease a 28cm (11-inch) closed springform pan; line base and side of pan with baking paper.

2 Stir prunes and brandy in a small saucepan, over medium heat; bring to the boil. Reduce heat, simmer, uncovered, 5 minutes; cool.

3 Melt chocolate in a medium heatproof bowl over a saucepan of simmering water (don't let the water touch the base of the bowl); stir until smooth. Cool.

4 Beat butter and sugar in a small bowl with an electric mixer until light and fluffy. Beat in eggs, one at a time. Transfer mixture to a large bowl; stir in prune mixture, ground almonds and melted chocolate.

5 Spread mixture into the pan; bake about 45 minutes. Cool cake in pan. Serve with cream, if you like.

serves 10
prep + cook time 1 hour (+ cooling) **storage** Cake will keep in an airtight container at room temperature for 3 days, or in the refrigerator for 1 week, or frozen for 2 months.

rich chocolate cake with strawberries & ganache

- 1½ cups (180g) ground almonds
- 200g (6½ ounces) butter, chopped
- 6 egg whites
- 1 cup (220g) caster (superfine) sugar
- ¼ cup (35g) self-raising flour
- 2 tablespoons cocoa powder
- 100g (3 ounces) dark eating (semi-sweet) chocolate, finely chopped
- 250g (8 ounces) strawberries, hulled, sliced
- 2 teaspoons icing (confectioners') sugar

chocolate ganache
- ½ cup (125ml) pouring cream
- 260g (8½ ounces) dark eating (semi-sweet) chocolate, chopped

1 Preheat oven to 160°C/325°F. Grease a deep 20cm (8-inch) round cake pan; line base with baking paper.

2 Spread ground almonds in a thin layer on an oven tray, roast about 8 minutes or until browned lightly. Cool.

3 Melt butter in a small saucepan over medium heat, about 5 minutes or until a dark brown colour. Strain immediately through a fine sieve, into a heatproof measuring jug – you'll need ⅔ cup melted butter.

4 Whisk egg whites in a medium bowl with a fork until combined. Whisk in almonds, sugar, sifted flour and cocoa. Gradually whisk warm butter into almond mixture; stir in chocolate.

5 Pour mixture into a pan. Bake cake about 55 minutes. Stand cake in pan 5 minutes before turning, top-side up, onto a wire rack to cool.

6 Meanwhile, make chocolate ganache. Place cake on a serving plate. Spread ganache over cake.

7 Arrange strawberries on top of the cake in layers to represent flower petals. Dust with sifted icing sugar just before serving.

chocolate ganache
Bring cream to the boil in a medium saucepan; remove from heat. Add chocolate to pan; stir until smooth. Refrigerate ganache about 30 minutes or until thickened.

serves 10
prep + cook time
1 hour 45 minutes
(+ cooling & refrigeration)
storage Cake will keep in an
airtight container in the
refrigerator for 3 days, or in
the freezer (without ganache
and strawberries) for 3 months.

tip It's important to measure the closed springform pan; the measurement appearing on the base of the springform pan sometimes refers to the measurement of the pan when it is open.

serves 12
prep + cook time 2 hours
(+ cooling & refrigeration)
storage Cake will keep in an airtight container at room temperature for 3 days, or in the refrigerator for 1 week, or frozen (without ganache and candied oranges) for 2 months.

brandy marmalade chocolate cake

- 200g (6½ ounces) dark eating (semi-sweet) chocolate, chopped
- 250g (8 ounces) butter, chopped
- 1½ cups (375ml) hot water
- 2 cups (440g) caster (superfine) sugar
- 1½ cups (225g) self-raising flour
- 1 cup (150g) plain (all-purpose) flour
- ¼ cup (25g) cocoa powder
- 2 eggs
- ½ cup (170g) orange marmalade
- 16 candied orange slices (200g)

brandy syrup
- ½ cup (110g) caster (superfine) sugar
- ½ cup (125ml) water
- ¼ cup (60ml) brandy

dark chocolate ganache
- ⅔ cup (160ml) pouring cream
- 200g (6½ ounces) dark eating (semi-sweet) chocolate, chopped

1 Preheat oven to 150°C/300°F. Grease a 24cm (9½-inch) closed springform pan; line base and side of pan with baking paper.

2 Meanwhile, combine chocolate, butter, the water and sugar into a medium saucepan. Stir over low heat until smooth. Transfer mixture to a large bowl; cool until mixture is barely warm.

3 Beat chocolate mixture on low speed with electric mixer for 1 minute. Beat in sifted dry ingredients, in three batches. Beat in eggs, one at a time.

4 Pour mixture into pan; bake 1¼ hours. Stand cake 5 minutes before turning, top-side up, onto wire rack to cool.

5 Meanwhile, make brandy syrup and dark chocolate ganache.

6 Split cake into three layers. Place one layer on a serving plate; brush with ¼ cup brandy syrup.

Spread with half the marmalade. Repeat layering with another cake layer, another ¼ cup syrup and the remaining marmalade. Top with remaining cake layer.

7 Spread dark chocolate ganache all over cake. Refrigerate about 30 minutes or until set. Top cake with candied oranges. Serve cake drizzled with remaining syrup and a little cream.

brandy syrup Stir sugar and the water in a small saucepan over high heat until sugar dissolves. Bring to the boil; remove from heat; cool. Stir in brandy.

dark chocolate ganache Bring cream to the boil in a medium saucepan; remove from heat. Add chocolate to pan; stir until smooth. Stand ganache about 15 minutes or until the mixture is spreadable.

flourless chocolate cake with mint toffee ice-cream

- 180g (5½ ounces) dark eating (semi-sweet) chocolate, chopped
- 100g (3 ounces) butter, chopped
- ⅓ cup (35g) cocoa powder
- ⅓ cup (80ml) hot water
- 1⅓ cups (300g) firmly packed brown sugar
- 1 cup (120g) ground almonds
- 4 eggs, separated
- 2 teaspoons cocoa powder, extra
- ¼ cup loosely packed fresh mint leaves
- 1.5 litres (6 cups) choc-mint ice-cream

toffee

- 1 cup (220g) caster (superfine) sugar
- ½ cup (125ml) water

serves 12
prep + cook time 1 hour 30 minutes (+ cooling)
storage Cake and toffee can be made a day ahead. Store in separate airtight containers.

1 Preheat oven to 160°C/325°F. Grease a deep 25cm (10-inch) round cake pan; line base and side of pan with baking paper.

2 Place chocolate and butter into a small saucepan; stir over low heat until smooth. Remove from heat.

3 Blend sifted cocoa with the water in a large bowl; whisk until smooth. Whisk in melted chocolate mixture, sugar, almonds and egg yolks until combined.

4 Beat egg whites in a small bowl with an electric mixer until soft peaks form. Fold into chocolate mixture, in two batches. Pour mixture into pan. Bake about 1 hour; cool cake in pan.

5 Meanwhile, make toffee.

6 Turn cake top-side up onto a board. Dust cake with sifted extra cocoa. Cut cake into wedges with a hot dry knife.

7 Process toffee and mint leaves until finely chopped. Serve cake with scoops of ice-cream and mint toffee.

toffee Grease oven tray. Combine sugar and the water in a small saucepan; stir over high heat, without boiling, until sugar dissolves. Bring to the boil; boil, uncovered, without stirring, about 12 minutes or until light caramel in colour. Pour toffee onto tray; cool. Break toffee into pieces.

tips A closed 25cm (10-inch) springform pan can be used to make this cake. Once the toffee is processed with the mint leaves, it will become sticky and must be used immediately.

date & chocolate torte

- 3 egg whites
- ½ cup (110g) caster (superfine) sugar
- 1 cup (140g) slivered almonds, chopped finely
- ¾ cup (115g) finely chopped dates
- 125g (4 ounces) dark eating (semi-sweet) chocolate, grated
- 300ml (½ pint) thickened (heavy) cream
- 50g (1½ ounce) piece dark eating (semi-sweet) chocolate, extra

1 Preheat oven to 160°C/325°F. Grease a 23cm (9-inch) springform pan; line base of pan with baking paper.

2 Beat egg whites in a small bowl with an electric mixer until soft peaks form. Gradually add sugar, beat until dissolved between additions. Fold in almonds, dates and grated chocolate. Spread mixture into pan.

3 Bake cake about 40 minutes or until firm; cool in pan. Remove pan ring and baking paper; turn, top-side up, onto a serving plate.

4 Beat cream in a small bowl with electric mixer until soft peaks form. Cover top of cake with whipped cream. Using a vegetable peeler, make curls from extra chocolate; sprinkle top of cake with curls. Refrigerate several hours before serving.

serves 12
prep + cook time 1 hour (+ cooling & refrigeration)
storage This torte is best served on the same day it is made.

sacher torte

- 150g (4½ ounces) dark eating (semi-sweet) chocolate, chopped
- 1 tablespoon water
- 150g (4½ ounces) butter, softened
- ½ cup (110g) caster (superfine) sugar
- 3 eggs, separated
- 1 cup (150g) plain (all-purpose) flour
- 2 tablespoons caster (superfine) sugar, extra
- 1 cup (320g) apricot jam, warmed, strained

chocolate icing

- 125g (4 ounces) dark eating (semi-sweet) chocolate, chopped
- 125g (4 ounces) butter, softened

serves 10
prep + cook time 1 hour 10 minutes (+ cooling & standing) storage Cake will keep in an airtight container for up to 3 days.

1 Preheat oven to 180°C/350°F. Grease a deep 22cm (8-inch) round cake pan; line base with baking paper.

2 Melt chocolate in a small heatproof bowl over a small saucepan of simmering water (do not allow water to touch base of bowl); stir in the water; cool mixture to room temperature.

3 Beat butter and sugar in a small bowl with an electric mixer until light and fluffy. Add egg yolks, one at a time, beating until combined. Transfer mixture to a large bowl; stir in chocolate mixture, then sifted flour.

4 Beat egg whites in a small bowl until soft peaks form, gradually beat in extra sugar, beating until dissolved between each addition; fold into chocolate mixture.

5 Spread mixture into pan. Bake about 30 minutes. Stand cake in pan 5 minutes before turning onto a wire rack to cool; leave cake upside-down.

6 Meanwhile, make chocolate icing.

7 Split cold cake in half; place one half, cut-side up, on serving plate. Brush half the warmed jam over cake half, top with remaining cake half. Brush cake all over with remaining jam. Stand about 1 hour at room temperature or until jam has set. Spread top and side of cake with icing; stand at room temperature until icing has set.

chocolate icing Melt chocolate and butter in a small heatproof bowl over a small saucepan of simmering water (do not allow water to touch base of bowl). Cool at room temperature until spreadable, stirring occasionally; this can take up to 2 hours.

serving suggestion
Serve with mixed berries.

tip This icing is also suitable for piping.

tip We used Frangelico for this recipe, but you can use any hazelnut or chocolate-flavoured liqueur you like.

hazelnut mud cake with fudge frosting

- 360g (11½ ounces) dark eating (semi-sweet) chocolate, chopped coarsely
- 225g (7 ounces) butter, chopped coarsely
- ¾ cup (165g) firmly packed brown sugar
- ¾ cup (180ml) water
- ¾ cup (110g) plain (all-purpose) flour
- ¼ cup (35g) self-raising flour
- ½ cup (50g) ground hazelnuts
- 2 eggs
- ⅓ cup (80ml) hazelnut-flavoured liqueur

fudge frosting
- 45g (1½ ounces) butter, chopped coarsely
- ⅓ cup (75g) firmly packed brown sugar
- 1 tablespoon water
- 2 tablespoons hazelnut-flavoured liqueur
- 1 cup (160g) icing (confectioners') sugar
- 2 tablespoons cocoa powder

1 Preheat oven to 150°C/300°F. Grease a deep 20cm (8-inch) round cake pan; line base and side with baking paper.
2 Stir chocolate, butter, sugar and the water in a medium saucepan over low heat until smooth. Transfer to a medium bowl; cool 15 minutes.
3 Stir sifted flours, ground hazelnuts, eggs and liqueur into chocolate mixture. Pour mixture into pan.
4 Bake cake about 1 hour 35 minutes. Stand in pan 5 minutes; turn, top-side up, onto a wire rack to cool.
5 Meanwhile, make fudge frosting.
6 Spread cake with fudge frosting.

fudge frosting Stir butter, brown sugar and the water in a small saucepan over heat, without boiling, until sugar dissolves. Remove from heat; stir in liqueur. Sift icing sugar and cocoa into a small bowl; gradually stir in hot butter mixture until smooth. Cover; refrigerate about 15 minutes or until frosting thickens. Beat frosting with a wooden spoon until spreadable.

serves 12
prep + cook time 2 hours (+ cooling)
storage This cake can be stored in an airtight container for up to 3 days. Unfrosted cake can be frozen for up to 3 months.

gluten-free chocolate cake

- 1 cup (125g) soy flour
- ¾ cup (110g) 100% maize cornflour (cornstarch)
- 1¼ teaspoons bicarbonate of soda (baking soda)
- ½ cup (50g) cocoa powder
- 1¼ cups (275g) caster (superfine) sugar
- 150g (4½ ounces) butter, melted
- 1 tablespoon white vinegar
- 1 cup (250ml) evaporated milk
- 2 eggs
- ½ cup mashed banana
- 2 tablespoons raspberry jam
- 300ml (½ pint) thickened cream, whipped

1 Preheat oven to 180°C/350°F. Grease two 22cm (9-inch) round sandwich cake pans; line bases with baking paper.

2 Sift dry ingredients into a large bowl; add butter, vinegar and evaporated milk. Beat with an electric mixer on low speed for 1 minute; add eggs, banana and jam, beat on medium speed for 2 minutes. Pour mixture into prepared pans.

3 Bake cakes about 30 minutes. Stand cakes in pans for 5 minutes; turn, top-side up, onto a wire rack to cool.

4 Sandwich cakes with whipped cream; lightly dust with extra sifted icing sugar, if you like.

serves 8
prep + cook time
50 minutes (+ cooling)
storage Cake will keep
refrigerated in an
airtight container for
up to 2 days. Cake not
suitable to freeze.

layered cakes

Layered cakes are as impressive in taste as they are in appearance, and often not as difficult to make as they look. Perfect for an afternoon tea, or for no particular reason at all.

serves 12
prep + cook time 1¾ hours
(+ refrigeration & cooling)
storage Cake will keep in an airtight
container in the refrigerator for
4 days, or in the freezer (without
filling or frosting) for 2 months.

lemon yoghurt cake with lemon curd frosting

- 250g (8 ounces) unsalted butter, chopped
- 2 tablespoons finely grated lemon rind
- 1½ cups (330g) caster (superfine) sugar
- 4 eggs
- 1½ cups (225g) self-raising flour
- ½ cup (75g) plain (all-purpose) flour
- ½ cup (140g) yoghurt
- ⅓ cup (80ml) lemon juice
- 250g (8 ounces) cream cheese
- 2 tablespoons flaked coconut

lemon curd

- 125g (4 ounces) unsalted butter, chopped
- 2 eggs
- 1 teaspoon finely grated lemon rind
- ⅓ cup (80ml) lemon juice
- ⅔ cup (150g) caster (superfine) sugar

1 Make lemon curd.

2 Preheat oven to 160°C/325°F. Grease deep 23cm (9-inch) round cake pan; line base and side with baking paper, extending paper 5cm (2-inches) above edge.

3 Beat butter, rind and sugar in a small bowl with an electric mixer until light and fluffy. Beat in eggs, one at a time. Transfer to a large bowl. Stir in sifted flours, yoghurt and juice in two batches.

4 Spread mixture into pan. Bake cake about 1½ hours. Stand cake in pan 5 minutes, before turning top-side up onto a wire rack to cool.

5 Meanwhile, beat cream cheese in a small bowl with electric mixer until creamy. Gradually beat in 1 cup of the lemon curd. Refrigerate, covered, about 30 minutes or until thickened.

6 Split cake into three layers. Place one layer on a serving plate, spread with one-third of the frosting, repeat layering; top cake with frosting. Pour remaining curd over top of cake; sprinkle with coconut.

lemon curd Combine butter, lightly beaten eggs, rind, juice and sugar in a small heavy-based saucepan; stir over low heat about 10 minutes or until mixture thickly coats the back of a wooden spoon. Strain curd, cover surface with plastic wrap. Refrigerate 2 hours until cold.

tip You need two large overripe bananas (460g) for this recipe.

banana caramel layer cake

- 185g (6 ounces) butter, softened
- 1¼ cup (175g) caster (superfine) sugar
- 3 eggs
- 2¼ cups (335g) self-raising flour
- ½ teaspoon bicarbonate of soda (baking soda)
- 1¼ cups mashed banana
- ⅓ cup (80ml) milk
- 380g (12 ounces) canned caramel Top 'n' Fill
- ¾ cup (180ml) thickened (heavy) cream, whipped
- 1 large (230g) banana, sliced thinly

1 Preheat oven to 180°C/350°F. Grease a 24cm (9½-inch) bundt pan, or 24cm (9½-inch) patterned silicone pan, well.

2 Beat butter and sugar in a small bowl with an electric mixer until light and fluffy. Beat in eggs, one at a time. Transfer mixture to a large bowl; stir in sifted dry ingredients, mashed banana and milk.

3 Spread mixture into pan; bake about 40 minutes. Stand cake in pan 5 minutes before turning onto a wire rack to cool.

4 Split cake into three layers. Spread bottom layer of cake with half the caramel, top with half the banana slices then half the cream. Repeat next layer using remaining caramel, banana slices and cream. Replace top of cake. Dust with icing (confectioners') sugar before serving, if you like.

serves 8
prep + cook time
1 hour 10 minutes
storage Cake will keep in
an airtight container in the
refrigerator for up to 3 days.
Cake (without filling) is suitable
to freeze.

serves 8
prep + cook time 50 minutes
storage Sponge will keep in
an airtight container in the
refrigerator for 2 days, or in
the freezer (without filling) for
1 month.

mango, coconut & mascarpone sponge

- 2 eggs
- ½ cup (110g) caster (superfine) sugar
- ⅓ cup (50g) wheaten cornflour (cornstarch)
- 1½ tablespoons custard powder (instant pudding mix)
- ½ teaspoon cream of tartar
- ¼ teaspoon bicarbonate of soda (baking soda)
- 2 tablespoons desiccated coconut
- 2 small mangoes (600g), sliced thinly

mascarpone filling

- 250g (8 ounces) cream cheese
- 90g (3 ounces) butter
- 200g (6½ ounces) mascarpone cheese
- 1 teaspoon coconut essence
- 1 cup (160g) icing (confectioners') sugar

1 Preheat oven to 180°C/350°F. Grease a 24cm x 32cm (9½-inch x 13-inch) swiss roll pan; line base and two long sides with baking paper, extending paper 5cm (2-inches) over long sides.

2 Beat eggs and ⅓ cup of the sugar in a small bowl with an electric mixer for about 8 minutes or until thick and creamy.

3 Meanwhile, triple sift cornflour, custard powder, cream of tartar and soda.

4 Fold cornflour mixture into egg mixture. Spread mixture evenly into pan; bake about 10 minutes.

5 Place a piece of baking paper, cut the same size as the pan, on a bench; sprinkle evenly with coconut and remaining sugar. Turn cake onto sugared paper; peel lining paper away.

6 Make the mascarpone filling.

7 Cut and discard edges from all sides of sponge, then cut crossways to make three rectangles. Place one sponge layer on a plate, sugar-side up; spread with 1 cup of the mascarpone filling, top with half of the mango. Repeat layering, top cake with remaining filling.

mascarpone filling

Beat cream cheese, butter, mascarpone and essence in medium bowl until light and fluffy. Beat in sifted icing sugar, in two batches.

black forest mud cake

- 200g (6½ ounces) dark eating (semi-sweet) chocolate, chopped coarsely
- 250g (8 ounces) butter, chopped
- ¾ cup (165g) caster (superfine) sugar
- ¾ cup (165g) firmly packed brown sugar
- 1 cup (250ml) hot water
- 1 tablespoon instant coffee granules
- 1½ cups (225g) plain (all-purpose) flour
- ¼ cup (35g) self-raising flour
- 2 tablespoons cocoa powder
- 2 eggs
- ⅓ cup (80ml) buttermilk
- ⅔ cup (160ml) thickened (heavy) cream, whipped
- 415g (13 ounces) canned black stoneless cherries, drained

dark chocolate ganache

- ⅔ cup (160ml) pouring cream
- 1 tablespoon cherry brandy
- 250g (8 ounces) dark eating (semi-sweet) chocolate

1 Preheat oven to 160°C/325°F. Grease a deep 22cm (9-inch) round cake pan; line base and side with baking paper.

2 Combine chocolate, butter, sugars, the water and coffee in a medium saucepan. Stir over low heat until smooth. Transfer mixture to a large bowl; cool 10 minutes.

3 Whisk sifted flours and cocoa, eggs and buttermilk into chocolate mixture.

4 Pour mixture into pan. Bake cake about 1 hour 20 minutes. Stand cake in pan 20 minutes before turning, top-side up, onto a wire rack to cool.

5 Meanwhile, make dark chocolate ganache and chocolate curls (see tip).

6 Split cake in half; spread base with half the ganache; top with whipped cream, cherries and top of cake. Spread cake top with remaining ganache, sprinkle with chocolate curls.

dark chocolate ganache Bring pouring cream and brandy to the boil in a medium saucepan; remove from heat. Add chocolate to pan; stir until smooth. Stand until thickened and spreadable.

serving suggestion Decorate with maraschino cherries, or you can use fresh or canned cherries, if you like.

serves 16
prep + cook time 1¾ hours
(+ standing & cooling)
storage Cake will keep in an airtight container at room temperature for 2 days, or in the refrigerator for 1 week, or in the freezer (without ganache) for 2 months.

tips Maraschino cherries are available from gourmet food stores and good delicatessens. To make chocolate curls, carefully drag a large sharp knife across the back of a chocolate block.

tip To make your own buttermilk equivalent, combine 1 tablespoon fresh lemon juice with enough reduced-fat milk to make 1 cup. Stand a few minutes until thickened; stir.

pink velvet cake

- 125g (4 ounces) butter, softened
- 1 teaspoon vanilla extract
- 1½ cups (330g) caster (superfine) sugar
- 2 eggs
- 1½ cups (225g) plain (all-purpose) flour
- 2 tablespoons cornflour (cornstarch)
- 2 tablespoons cocoa powder
- 1 cup (250ml) buttermilk
- 1 tablespoon rose pink food colouring
- 1 teaspoon white vinegar
- 1 teaspoon bicarbonate of soda (baking soda)
- 1 cup (50g) flaked coconut

mascarpone frosting

- 250g (8 ounces) cream cheese, softened
- 250g (8 ounces) mascarpone cheese
- 1 cup (160g) icing (confectioners') sugar
- 1 teaspoon vanilla extract
- 300ml (½ pint) thickened (heavy) cream

1 Preheat oven to 180°C/350°F. Grease two deep 23cm (9-inch) round cake pans; line bases and sides with baking paper.

2 Beat butter, extract, sugar and eggs in a small bowl with an electric mixer until light and fluffy. Transfer mixture to a large bowl; stir in sifted flours and cocoa and combined buttermilk and colouring, in two batches.

3 Combine vinegar and soda in a cup; allow to fizz, fold into cake mixture. Divide mixture between pans.

4 Bake cakes about 25 minutes. Stand cakes 10 minutes before turning, top-side up, onto a wire rack to cool. Wrap cakes in plastic wrap; freeze for 40 minutes.

5 Meanwhile, make mascarpone frosting.

6 Split cooled cakes in half. Place one layer on a serving plate, cut-side up; spread with ⅔ cup frosting. Repeat layering, finishing with remaining frosting spread over top and side of cake; press coconut onto side of cake.

mascarpone frosting

Beat cream cheese, mascarpone, sugar and extract in a small bowl with an electric mixer until smooth. Beat in cream until thickened.

serves 12
prep + cook time 1 hour (+ freezing)
storage Cake will keep in an airtight container in the refrigerator for 2 days. Cake (without filling or frosting) is suitable to freeze.

tiramisu torte

- **6 eggs**
- **1 cup (220g) caster (superfine) sugar**
- **½ cup (75g) plain (all-purpose) flour**
- **½ cup (75g) self-raising flour**
- **½ cup (75g) cornflour (cornstarch)**
- **¼ cup (10g) instant coffee powder**
- **1½ cups (375ml) boiling water**
- **¾ cup (180ml) marsala**
- **¼ cup (60ml) coffee-flavoured liqueur**
- **300ml (½ pint) thickened (heavy) cream**
- **½ cup (80g) icing (confectioners') sugar**
- **750g (1½ ounces) mascarpone cheese**
- **500g (1 pound) vienna almonds, chopped coarsely**

1 Preheat oven to 180°C/350°F. Grease two deep 22cm (9-inch) round cake pans; line bases with baking paper.

2 Beat eggs in a medium bowl with an electric mixer about 10 minutes or until thick and creamy. Add caster sugar, about 1 tablespoon at a time, beating until sugar is dissolved between additions. Gently fold triple-sifted flours into egg mixture. Divide cake mixture evenly between prepared pans.

3 Bake cakes about 25 minutes. Turn cakes top-side up onto wire racks to cool.

4 Meanwhile, dissolve coffee powder in the water in a small heatproof bowl. Stir in marsala and liqueur; cool.

5 Beat cream and icing sugar in a small bowl with an electric mixer until soft peaks form; transfer to a large bowl. Stir in mascarpone and ½-cup of the coffee mixture.

6 Split cooled cakes in half. Centre half of one cake on a serving plate; brush with a quarter of the remaining coffee mixture then spread with about 1 cup of the mascarpone cream. Repeat layering until last cake half is covered with mascarpone cream. Spread remaining mascarpone cream around side of cake; press almonds into side and top of cake. Refrigerate until ready to serve.

serves 12
prep + cook time 55 minutes (+ cooling) **storage** This cake is best made a day ahead and kept refrigerated in an airtight container. Cake (without filling) is suitable to freeze for up to 1 month.

torta di mamma

- 280g (9-ounce) packet sponge cake mix
- 1 cup (250ml) strong black coffee
- ⅓ cup (80ml) coffee liqueur
- ⅓ cup (80ml) brandy
- 1 tablespoon caster (superfine) sugar

custard filling
- ½ cup (75g) cornflour (cornstarch)
- ½ cup (60g) custard powder (instant pudding mix)
- ½ cup (110g) caster (superfine) sugar
- 2½ cups (625ml) milk
- 1½ cups (375ml) pouring cream
- 2 teaspoons vanilla extract
- 30g (1 ounce) butter
- 2 egg yolks
- 90g (3 ounces) dark eating (semi-sweet) chocolate, melted

serves 12
prep + cook time 1 hour 50 minutes (+ refrigeration)
storage Cake will keep for up to 3 days in an airtight container in the refrigerator.

1 Preheat oven to 160°C/325°F. Grease a deep 22cm (9-inch) round cake pan; line base with baking paper.
2 Make sponge cake according to directions on the packet; pour mixture into pan. Bake about 35 minutes. Turn cake onto a wire rack to cool.
3 Meanwhile, make custard filling.
4 Combine cold coffee, liqueur, brandy and sugar in a small jug; mix well. Split cooled cake into four layers. Place first layer on a serving plate; brush well with the coffee mixture.
5 Spread half the plain custard over cake. Top custard with second layer of cake; brush with coffee mixture. Spread a third of the chocolate custard over cake. Place third layer of cake on top of custard; brush with coffee mixture then spread with remaining plain custard.

Top with fourth layer of cake; brush with coffee mixture.
6 Spread remaining chocolate custard over top and side of cake; refrigerate 3 hours or overnight.

custard filling Combine cornflour, custard powder and sugar in a medium saucepan. Gradually add combined milk, cream and extract; stir over low heat until mixture boils and thickens. Add butter; simmer, stirring, 3 minutes. Remove pan from heat; stir in egg yolks. Place custard in a large bowl; cover with plastic wrap. Cool. Divide custard mixture between two bowls. Stir melted chocolate into one, leave remaining custard plain.

serves 16
prep + cook time
1 hour 30 minutes
storage Cake (without
praline) will keep in
an airtight container in
the refrigerator for up
to 3 days.

chocolate chiffon cake

- ½ cup (50g) cocoa powder
- ¾ cup (180ml) boiling water
- 2 cups (300g) self-raising flour
- 1½ cups (330g) caster (superfine) sugar
- 7 eggs, separated
- ½ cup (125ml) vegetable oil
- 1 teaspoon vanilla extract

walnut praline

- 1 cup (220g) caster (superfine) sugar
- ½ cup (50g) walnuts
- 60g (2 ounces) dark eating (semi-sweet) chocolate, chopped

brandied buttercream

- 190g (6 ounces) butter, softened
- 3 cups (480g) icing (confectioners') sugar
- ¼ cup (25g) cocoa powder
- ¼ cup (60ml) brandy

1 Preheat oven to 180°C/350°F. Grease a deep 22cm (9-inch) round cake pan; cover base and side with baking paper.

2 Blend cocoa with the water in a small bowl; cool. Beat sifted flour and sugar, cocoa mixture, egg yolks, oil and extract in a large bowl with an electric mixer until mixture is smooth and has changed in colour.

3 Beat egg whites in a large bowl with an electric mixer until soft peaks form; fold into cocoa mixture in four batches.

4 Pour mixture into a pan; bake about 1 hour or until firm. Stand cake 5 minutes before turning, top-side up, onto a wire rack to cool.

5 Make walnut praline.

6 Make brandied buttercream.

7 Split cold cake into three layers; join layers with buttercream. Spread cake evenly with remaining buttercream. Decorate with walnut praline.

walnut praline Place sugar in a heavy-based frying pan; cook over low heat, without stirring, until sugar is melted and golden brown. Add nuts; pour onto greased oven tray; cool. Blend or process praline with chocolate until finely chopped.

brandied buttercream Beat butter in a small bowl with an electric mixer until pale; beat in sifted icing sugar, cocoa, then brandy.

tip You can replace the walnuts with hazelnuts or pecans, if you like.

feather-light cakes

These light-as-a-feather cakes are lovely and delicate.
They're ideal served with tea and coffee. In fact they are
so airy and weightless you might as well have two pieces.

tips Do not grease the tube pan; the cake mixture needs to cling to the pan as it rises. The pan is measured at the top, not the base. If the cake doesn't drop from the pan when it becomes cold, gently ease it from the side and/or base using a metal spatula.

caramel angel food cake with sugared pecans

- ½ cup (75g) plain (all-purpose) flour
- ½ cup (75g) wheaten cornflour (cornstarch)
- 2 teaspoons ground cinnamon
- 1¼ cups (275g) firmly packed brown sugar
- 12 egg whites
- 1 teaspoon cream of tartar
- 1 teaspoon vanilla extract
- 1 cup (120g) pecan halves
- 1 teaspoon cinnamon sugar

caramel cream cheese frosting
- ¼ cup (55g) firmly packed brown sugar
- 80g (2½ ounces) butter
- ⅓ cup (80ml) thickened (heavy) cream
- 500g (1 pound) cream cheese
- 1½ cups (240g) icing (confectioners') sugar

serves 16
prep + cook time
1 hour (+ cooling)
storage Cake will keep in an airtight container at room temperature for 1 day, or in the refrigerator for 2 days, or in the freezer for 1 month.

1 Preheat oven to 180°C/350°F.

2 Sift flours, ground cinnamon and ¼ cup of the sugar together six times.

3 Beat egg whites in a large bowl with an electric mixer until foamy; beat in cream of tartar. Gradually add remaining sugar to egg mixture, beating until dissolved between additions. Add extract; beat until firm peaks form. Use a large metal spoon to gently fold in the flour mixture.

4 Spread mixture into ungreased 25cm (10-inch) tube pan; smooth surface. Bake about 30 minutes.

5 Place a piece of baking paper, cut larger than the pan, on a bench; turn pan upside down onto bench over baking paper. Do not move or bump the pan while the cake is cooling. The cake will drop from the pan when cold.

6 Make caramel cream cheese frosting.

7 Split cake in half, place one layer on a serving plate, cut-side up; spread with 1 cup of the frosting; top with remaining cake layer. Spread remaining frosting all over cake; top with pecans, sprinkle with cinnamon sugar.

caramel cream cheese frosting Combine brown sugar and butter in a small saucepan; stir over heat until sugar is dissolved. Bring to the boil. Remove from heat; whisk in cream until smooth. Cool to room temperature. Beat cream cheese in a large bowl with an electric mixer until smooth; beat in butter mixture and sifted icing sugar, in two batches.

devil's food cake

- 180g (5½ ounces) butter, softened
- 1¾ cups (385g) caster (superfine) sugar
- 3 eggs
- 1½ cups (225g) self-raising flour
- ½ cup (75g) plain (all-purpose) flour
- ½ teaspoon bicarbonate of soda (baking soda)
- ⅔ cup (70g) cocoa powder
- 3 teaspoons instant coffee granules
- ½ cup (125ml) water
- ½ cup (125ml) milk
- ½ teaspoon red food colouring
- 300ml (½ pint) thickened (heavy) cream, whipped

rich chocolate frosting
- 60g (2 ounces) dark eating (semi-sweet) chocolate, chopped
- 60g (2 ounces) butter, chopped

1 Preheat oven to 180°C/350°F. Grease two deep 20cm (8-inch) round cake pans; line bases with baking paper.

2 Beat butter and sugar in a small bowl with an electric mixer until light and fluffy; beat in eggs, one at a time.

3 Transfer mixture to a large bowl; in two batches, fold in sifted flours, soda and cocoa powder with combined coffee, the water, milk and colouring.

4 Pour mixture into pans; bake about 45 minutes. Stand cakes in pan 5 minutes before turning, top-side up, onto wire racks to cool.

5 Meanwhile, make rich chocolate frosting.

6 Sandwich cold cakes with whipped cream; top with frosting.

rich chocolate frosting
Combine chocolate and butter in a small heatproof bowl over a small saucepan of simmering water (water should not touch base of bowl); stir until smooth. Remove from heat. Cool at room temperature, stirring occasionally, until frosting is spreadable.

serves 10
prep + cook time 1 hour (+ cooling)
storage Cake (without filling) will keep in an airtight container in the refrigerator for 2 days, or in the freezer (without filling or icing) for 1 month.

tips Do not grease the tube pan; the cake mixture needs to cling to the pan as it rises. The pan is measured at the top, not the base. If the cake doesn't drop from the pan when it becomes cold, gently ease it from the side and/or base using a metal spatula.

raspberry chiffon cake

- 4 eggs, separated
- ¼ teaspoon cream of tartar
- 1 cup (150g) self-raising flour
- ¾ cup (165g) caster (superfine) sugar
- 9g (½-ounce) packet sugar-free raspberry jelly crystals
- ½ cup (125ml) water
- ¼ cup (60ml) vegetable oil
- 1 cup (250ml) thickened (heavy) cream
- 1 tablespoon icing (confectioners') sugar

raspberry icing
- 125g (4 ounces) fresh raspberries
- 2 cups (320g) icing (confectioners') sugar
- 15g (½ ounce) butter, melted
- 1 tablespoon hot water, approximately

> **serves** 16 **prep + cook time** 1¼ hours (+ cooling)
> **storage** Cake will keep in an airtight container in the refrigerator for 2 days, or in the freezer (without filling or icing) for 1 month.

1 Preheat oven to 180°C/350°F.
2 Beat egg whites and cream of tartar in a small bowl with an electric mixer until firm peaks form.
3 Sift flour six times.
4 Combine flour, sugar, jelly crystals, the water, oil and egg yolks in a large bowl; whisk until smooth. Fold in egg white mixture, in two batches.
5 Spread mixture into an ungreased 25cm (10-inch) tube pan; smooth surface. Bake about 50 minutes.
6 Place a piece of baking paper, cut larger than the pan, on the bench; turn pan upside down onto bench over baking paper. Do not move or bump the pan while the cake is cooling. The cake will drop from the pan when cold.
7 Make raspberry icing.

8 Beat cream and sifted icing sugar in a small bowl with an electric mixer until soft peaks form.
9 Split cake in half, place one layer on a serving plate, cut-side up; spread with cream, top with remaining cake layer. Drizzle cake with icing; decorate with reserved raspberries.

raspberry icing
Push one-third of the raspberries through a fine sieve into a small heatproof bowl; discard seeds. Reserve remaining raspberries to decorate cake. Sift icing sugar into the same bowl; stir in butter and enough of the water to make a thick paste. Place bowl over a small saucepan of simmering water; stir until icing is spreadable.

marbled victoria sponge

- 250g (8 ounces) unsalted butter
- 1 cup (220g) caster (superfine) sugar
- 1 teaspoon vanilla extract
- 4 eggs
- 1⅔ cups (250g) self-raising flour
- ⅓ cup (80ml) milk
- 2 tablespoons cocoa powder
- 2 tablespoons milk, extra

chocolate buttercream
- 125g (4 ounces) butter
- ⅓ cup (35g) Milo powder
- 2 tablespoons cocoa powder
- 1 teaspoon vanilla extract
- 1½ cups (240g) icing (confectioners') sugar
- ⅓ cup (80ml) thickened (heavy) cream

1 Preheat oven to 180°C/350°F. Grease two deep 20cm (8-inch) round cake pans; line bases with baking paper.
2 Beat butter, sugar and extract in a small bowl with an electric mixer until light and fluffy. Beat in eggs, one at a time. Transfer mixture to a large bowl. Fold in sifted flour and milk, in two batches.
3 Blend cocoa powder with extra milk in a small bowl; fold cocoa mixture into cake mixture to give a marbled effect.
4 Divide mixture between pans; smooth surface. Bake about 30 minutes. Turn cakes, top-side up, onto baking-paper-lined wire rack to cool.

5 Make chocolate buttercream.
6 Sandwich cakes with half the buttercream; spread remaining buttercream over top of cake.
chocolate buttercream Beat butter, Milo, sifted cocoa and extract in a small bowl with an electric mixer until light and fluffy. Beat in sifted icing sugar, in two batches; beat in cream until thickened.

serves 12
prep + cook time 50 minutes (+ cooling)
storage Sponge will keep in an airtight container in the refrigerator for 2 days, or in the freezer (without filling or icing) for 1 month.

mocha spice sponge cake

- 4 eggs
- ¾ cup (165g) firmly packed dark brown sugar
- ¾ cup (105g) wheaten cornflour (cornstarch)
- ¼ cup (25g) cocoa powder
- 1 teaspoon ground cinnamon
- 1 teaspoon cream of tartar
- ½ teaspoon bicarbonate of soda (baking soda)
- 2 teaspoons instant coffee granules
- 1 teaspoon hot water

cinnamon cream
- 1 cup (250ml) thickened (heavy) cream
- 2 teaspoons cinnamon sugar

chocolate icing
- 1 cup (160g) icing (confectioners') sugar
- 2 tablespoons cocoa powder
- 10g (½ ounce) butter
- 2 tablespoons hot water

1 Preheat oven to 180°C/350°F. Grease two deep 22cm (9-inch) round cake pans.

2 Beat eggs and sugar in a small bowl with an electric mixer for about 10 minutes or until thick and creamy. Transfer to a large bowl.

3 Meanwhile, triple sift the dry ingredients, except for the coffee.

4 Gently fold dry ingredients into egg mixture, then fold in combined coffee and the water.

5 Divide mixture evenly between pans; bake about 20 minutes. Turn sponges, top-side up, onto baking-paper-lined wire racks to cool.

6 Meanwhile, make cinnamon cream and chocolate icing.

7 Sandwich sponges with cinnamon cream; drizzle with chocolate icing.

cinnamon cream Beat ingredients in a small bowl with an electric mixer until soft peaks form.

chocolate icing Sift icing sugar and cocoa powder into a medium heatproof bowl; add combined butter and the water, stir until icing is pourable.

serves 12
prep + cook time 45 minutes (+ cooling)
storage Sponge will keep in an airtight container in the refrigerator for 2 days, or in the freezer (without filling or icing) for 1 month.

honey spice sponge cake

- **2 eggs**
- **½ cup (110g) caster (superfine) sugar**
- **⅓ cup (50g) wheaten cornflour (cornstarch)**
- **1½ tablespoons custard powder (instant pudding mix)**
- **1 teaspoon mixed spice**
- **½ teaspoon cream of tartar**
- **¼ teaspoon bicarbonate of soda (baking soda)**
- **300ml (½ pint) thickened (heavy) cream**
- **2 tablespoons honey**
- **1 tablespoon icing (confectioners') sugar**

serves 6
prep + cook time 30 minutes
storage Sponge (without filling) will keep in an airtight container in the refrigerator for 2 days, or in the freezer (without filling) for 1 month.

1 Preheat oven to 180°C/350°F. Grease a 25cm x 30cm (10-inch x 12-inch) swiss roll pan; line base and long sides with baking paper, extending paper 5cm (2-inch) over sides.
2 Beat eggs and ⅓ cup of the sugar in a small bowl with an electric mixer about 10 minutes or until thick and creamy.
3 Meanwhile, triple-sift dry ingredients; fold into egg mixture. Spread mixture into pan; bake 10 minutes.
4 Place a piece of baking paper, cut the same size as the pan, on bench; sprinkle evenly with remaining sugar. Turn hot sponge onto paper; peel away lining paper. Cool; trim all sides of sponge.

5 Beat cream and honey in a small bowl with an electric mixer until firm peaks form.
6 Cut sponge widthways into three equal-sized rectangles. Place one piece of sponge on a serving plate; spread with half the cream mixture. Top with the second piece of sponge and remaining cream. Finish with remaining sponge piece, then dust with sifted icing sugar.

serves 10
prep + cook time
50 minutes (+ standing time)
storage Cake will keep in an
airtight container in the
refrigerator for 2 days, or in
the freezer (without filling or
icing) for 1 month.

tips Do not grease the tube pan; the cake mixture needs to cling to the pan as it rises. The pan is measured at the top, not the base. If the cake doesn't drop from the pan when it becomes cold, gently ease it from the side and/or base using a metal spatula.

angel food cake

- ½ cup (75g) plain (all-purpose) flour
- ½ cup (75g) wheaten cornflour (cornstarch)
- 1¼ cups (275g) caster (superfine) sugar
- ¼ teaspoon salt
- 12 egg whites
- 1 teaspoon cream of tartar
- 1 teaspoon vanilla extract

1 Preheat oven to 180°C/350°F.

2 Sift flours, ¼ cup of the sugar and the salt together six times.

3 Beat egg whites in a large bowl with an electric mixer until foamy; beat in cream of tartar. Gradually add remaining sugar to egg mixture, beating until dissolved between additions. Add extract; beat until firm peaks form. Use a large metal spoon to gently fold in the flour mixture.

4 Spread mixture into an ungreased 25cm (10-inch) tube pan; smooth surface. Bake about 30 minutes.

5 Place a piece of baking paper, cut larger than the pan, on bench; turn pan upside down onto bench over baking paper. Do not move or bump the pan while the cake is cooling. The cake will drop from the pan when cold. Decorate with fresh berries, if you like.

cream cheese lemon cake

- 185g (6 ounces) butter, softened
- 185g (6 ounces) cream cheese, softened
- 1 tablespoon finely grated lemon rind
- 1½ cups (330g) caster (superfine) sugar
- 3 eggs
- 1 cup (150g) self-raising flour
- ⅔ cup (100g) plain (all-purpose) flour

1 Preheat oven to 180°C/350°F. Grease a 20cm (8-inch) baba pan.
2 Beat butter, cream cheese and rind together in a small bowl with an electric mixer until light in colour. Add sugar; beat until light and fluffy. Beat in eggs, one at a time, until just combined.
3 Add sifted flours, in two batches; beat on a low speed until just combined. Spoon mixture into prepared pan.
4 Bake cake about 1 hour. Stand cake in pan 10 minutes before turning, top-side up, onto a wire rack to cool. Dust cake with a little sifted icing sugar, if you like.

tips Lemon rind can be substituted with another citrus rind, such as orange, lime or mandarin, or you can use 1 teaspoon of your favourite essence rather than the citrus rind. Cover cake loosely with foil about halfway during baking time if it starts to overbrown.

serves 16
prep + cook time
1 hour 15 minutes
storage Cake will keep
well in an airtight container
for up to 1 week at room
temperature or even longer
in an airtight container in
the refrigerator. Cake can be
frozen for up to 3 months.

celebration cakes

Nothing says celebration quite like a show-stopper cake.
This chapter is full of cakes that are perfect for every special
occasion — engagements, Christmas, and of course birthdays.

candied citrus cake

- 250g (8 ounces) butter, softened
- 1 tablespoon each finely grated orange & lemon rind
- 1½ cups (330g) caster (superfine) sugar
- 4 eggs
- 1½ cups (225g) self-raising flour
- ½ cup (75g) plain (all-purpose) flour
- ½ cup (125ml) orange juice
- ¼ cup (60ml) lemon juice

candied citrus

- 1 cup (220g) caster (superfine) sugar
- ½ cup (125ml) water
- 1 medium orange (240g), sliced thinly
- 1 medium lime (75g), sliced thinly

filling

- 300g (9½ ounces) mascarpone cheese
- 300g (9½ ounces) crème fraîche
- 1 tablespoon icing (confectioners') sugar
- 2 teaspoons finely grated orange rind

glacé icing

- 2 cups (320g) icing (confectioners') sugar
- 2½ tablespoons boiling water

1 Preheat oven to 160°C/325°F. Grease a deep 22cm (9-inch) round cake pan; line base and side with baking paper.
2 Beat butter, rinds and sugar in a large bowl with an electric mixer until light and fluffy. Beat in eggs, one at a time. Fold in sifted flours and juices, in two batches; spread mixture into pan.
3 Bake cake 1 hour 10 minutes. Stand cake in pan 10 minutes before turning, top-side up, onto a wire rack to cool.
4 Meanwhile, make candied citrus, filling and glacé icing.
5 Split cake into two layers; sandwich with filling.
6 Drizzle cake with glacé icing. Just before serving, top with candied citrus.

candied citrus Combine sugar and the water in a large frying pan. Stir over low heat, without boiling, until sugar dissolves; add orange and lime slices. Bring to the boil. Reduce heat to low; simmer, uncovered, 15 minutes, turning slices occasionally. Remove from heat; cool slices on a wire rack.
filling Beat ingredients in a small bowl with electric mixer until soft peaks form.
glacé icing Sift icing sugar into heatproof bowl; add boiling water, stir until smooth.

serves 8
prep + cook time 1 hour 45 minutes
storage Cake will keep in an airtight container at room temperature for up to 4 days. Cake (without filling and glaze) is suitable to freeze.

tip You will need about three oranges, one lemon and one lime for this cake.

serves 36
prep + cook time
3¼ hours (+ cooling)
storage Cake can be made
up to 6 months ahead; store
in an airtight container in
the refrigerator, or freeze
for up to 12 months.

whiskey fruit cake

- 2 cups (300g) raisins, chopped coarsely
- 1 cup (150g) dried apricots, chopped coarsely
- ¾ cup (150g) red glacé cherries, chopped coarsely
- 1½ cups (240g) sultanas
- 1 cup (160g) dried currants
- ¾ cup (180ml) water
- ½ cup (125ml) whiskey
- 250g (8 ounces) butter, chopped
- 1 cup (220g) firmly packed brown sugar
- ½ teaspoon bicarbonate of soda (baking soda)
- 4 eggs, lightly beaten
- 1¼ cups (185g) self-raising flour
- 1¼ cups (185g) plain (all-purpose) flour
- ½ cup (60g) pecans
- ⅓ cup (55g) blanched almonds
- ¼ cup (45g) roasted pistachios
- 2 tablespoons whiskey, extra

1 Preheat oven to 150°C/300°F. Grease deep 22cm (9-inch) round cake pan; line base and side with two thicknesses of baking paper, extending 5cm (2-inches) above edge.

2 Combine raisins, apricots, cherries, sultanas, currants, the water, whiskey, chopped butter, sugar and soda in a large saucepan; stir over medium heat until butter is melted and sugar dissolved. Bring to the boil; remove from heat. Transfer to a large bowl; cool to room temperature. Stir eggs into fruit mixture, then stir in sifted flours.

3 Spread mixture evenly into pan. Tap on bench; level top. Scatter with combined nuts, pressing in slightly. Bake cake about 2 hours 40 minutes.

4 Brush hot cake with extra whiskey. Cover hot cake with foil; cool cake in pan overnight.

chocolate & strawberry meringue gateau

- 125g (4 ounces) butter, softened
- 4 eggs, separated
- ¾ cup (165g) caster (superfine) sugar
- 1 cup (150g) self-raising flour
- ⅓ cup (35g) cocoa powder
- ½ teaspoon bicarbonate of soda (baking soda)
- 1 cup (250ml) buttermilk
- ⅓ cup (150g) caster (superfine) sugar, extra
- ¼ cup (30g) coarsely chopped roasted hazelnuts
- ⅔ cup (160ml) thickened (heavy) cream
- 1 tablespoon icing (confectioners') sugar
- 250g (8 ounces) strawberries, halved

1 Preheat oven to 160°C/325°F. Grease two 20cm (8-inch) round cake pans; line bases and sides with baking paper.

2 Beat butter, egg yolks and caster sugar in a medium bowl with an electric mixer until light and fluffy. Stir in combined sifted flour, cocoa and soda, then buttermilk. Divide mixture between pans.

3 Beat egg whites in a small bowl with an electric mixer until soft peaks form; gradually add extra caster sugar, one tablespoon at a time, beating until sugar dissolves between the additions.

4 Divide meringue mixture over cake mixture in pans; using a spatula, spread meringue so cake mixture is completely covered. Sprinkle nuts over meringue mixture on one of the cakes.

5 Bake cakes for 25 minutes. Cover pans loosely with foil; bake a further 20 minutes. Stand cake in pan 5 minutes before turning, top-side up, onto a wire rack to cool.

6 Beat cream and icing sugar in a small bowl with an electric mixer until soft peaks form. Place cake without nuts on a serving plate; spread with cream mixture. Top with strawberries, then remaining cake.

serves 12
prep + cook time 1½ hours (+ cooling)
storage This recipe is best made on the day of serving.

tip We painted a branch of real holly roughly with melted dark chocolate to make the (inedible) decoration on the cake.

rich chocolate fruit cake

- 850g (1¾ pounds) canned seeded black cherries in syrup
- 1 cup (150g) raisins, chopped coarsely
- ¾ cup (120g) finely chopped seeded dried dates
- ½ cup (80g) sultanas
- ½ cup (95g) finely chopped seeded prunes
- 1 cup (200g) dried figs, chopped finely
- 1 cup (250ml) marsala
- 1 cup (120g) pecans
- 185g (6 ounces) butter, softened
- 2 teaspoons finely grated orange rind
- 1¼ cups (275g) firmly packed dark brown sugar
- 3 eggs
- 1¼ cups (185g) plain (all-purpose) flour
- ½ cup (75g) self-raising flour
- 2 tablespoons cocoa powder
- 2 teaspoons mixed spice
- 100g (3 ounces) dark eating (semi-sweet) chocolate, chopped finely

ganache
- 200g (6½ ounces) dark eating (semi-sweet) chocolate, chopped coarsely
- ½ cup (125ml) pouring cream

1 Drain cherries; reserve ⅓ cup syrup. Quarter cherries. Combine cherries with remaining fruit, ¾ cup of the marsala and reserved cherry syrup in a large bowl. Cover; stand overnight.

2 Preheat oven to 150°C/300°F. Grease a deep 22cm (9-inch) round cake pan; line with two layers of baking paper, extending it 5cm (2 inches) over the edge of the pan.

3 Process half the pecans until ground finely; chop the remaining pecans coarsely.

4 Beat butter, rind and sugar in a small bowl with an electric mixer until combined; beat in eggs, one at a time. Mix butter mixture into fruit mixture; stir in sifted dry ingredients, chocolate and ground and chopped nuts. Spread mixture into pan.

5 Bake cake about 3 hours. Brush hot cake with remaining marsala, cover with foil; cool in pan.

6 Make ganache.

7 Turn cake out onto serving plate. Spread with ganache. Top with chocolate decoration (see tip). Dust with sifted icing (confectioners') sugar to serve, if you like.

ganache Stir ingredients in a small saucepan over low heat until smooth. Refrigerate, stirring occasionally, about 20 minutes or until spreadable.

> **serves** 20
> **prep + cook time**
> 4 hours (+ standing & refrigeration) **storage**
> Cake (without icing) can be kept in the fridge for up to 3 months or frozen for 12 months. Once iced, the cake can be stored in the fridge for 2 weeks. Cut and bring to room temperature before serving.

lemon curd meringue cake with blueberries

- 1 cup (150g) almond kernels
- 4 egg whites
- 1 cup (220g) caster (superfine) sugar
- 125g (4 ounces) white eating chocolate
- 600ml (1 pint) double (thick) cream
- 125g (4 ounces) fresh blueberries

lemon curd

- 250g (8 ounces) cold butter
- 2 eggs
- ⅔ cup (160ml) lemon juice
- 1⅓ cups (300g) caster (superfine) sugar
- 2 egg yolks

serves 12
prep + cook time
1¾ hours (+ refrigeration, cooling & standing)
storage Cake will keep in refrigerator for up to 2 days.

1 Make lemon curd.

2 Preheat oven to 160°C/325°F. Grease a 24cm (9½-inch) closed springform pan; insert base of pan upside down to make cake easier to remove. Line base with baking paper.

3 Spread almonds, in a single layer, on an oven tray; roast, uncovered, about 12 minutes or until skins begin to split; cool. Chop finely.

4 Beat egg whites and ¼ cup of the sugar in a small bowl with an electric mixer until firm peaks form. Add remaining sugar; beat on high speed about 5 minutes or until sugar is dissolved.

5 Meanwhile, coarsely grate chocolate; fold into meringue mixture with nuts. Spread mixture into pan. Bake about 40 minutes. Cool meringue in pan.

6 Beat half the cream in a small bowl with an electric mixer until soft peaks form; fold in lemon curd.

7 Spoon curd mixture onto meringue. Refrigerate several hours or overnight until firm.

8 Top cake with remaining cream and blueberries (see tip for how to make toffee blueberries) just before serving.

lemon curd Chop butter; place in a medium saucepan. Lightly beat eggs in a small bowl; strain into pan. Add remaining ingredients; stir over low heat, without boiling, about 10 minutes or until mixture thickly coats the back of a wooden spoon. Transfer curd to a medium heatproof bowl. Cover; refrigerate until cold.

tip To make the toffee-dipped blueberries, stir 1 cup white sugar with ½ cup water over medium heat until sugar is dissolved. Bring to the boil; boil, without stirring, until sugar has thickened and turns a caramel colour. Push a wooden toothpick into each blueberry. Remove toffee from heat; allow bubbles to subside. Working with one blueberry at a time, hold berry by the toothpick, dip into the thickened toffee. Hold blueberry above the toffee so that a trail of toffee falls from the berry. Hold upside down until starting to set, then place onto cake. You may need to reheat the toffee if it starts to thicken too much.

tip Tokay is a sweet white fortified wine.

gluten-free dairy-free spicy fruit cake

- 1¼ cups (200g) sultanas
- 1 cup (150g) finely chopped seeded dried dates
- 1 cup (150g) raisins, chopped coarsely
- ¾ cup (120g) dried currants
- 1 cup (250g) coarsely chopped glacé apricots
- 1 cup (250ml) tokay
- 185g (6 ounces) dairy-free margarine
- 1 cup (220g) firmly packed dark brown sugar
- 3 eggs
- 1 cup (120g) ground almonds
- 1½ cups (270g) rice flour
- 1 teaspoon cream of tartar
- 1 teaspoon ground nutmeg
- ½ teaspoon bicarbonate of soda (baking soda)
- ½ teaspoon each ground ginger and ground cloves

1 Combine fruit and ¾ cup of the tokay in a large bowl, cover with plastic wrap; stand overnight.

2 Preheat oven to 120°C/250°F. Line a deep 22cm (9-inch) round cake pan with two layers of baking paper, extending paper 5cm (2 inches) above side.

3 Beat margarine and sugar in a small bowl with an electric mixer until combined; beat in eggs, one at a time. Mix margarine mixture into fruit mixture; mix in ground almonds and sifted dry ingredients. Spread mixture into pan.

4 Bake cake about 2½ hours. Brush hot cake with remaining tokay, cover with foil; cool in pan. Turn cake out onto a serving plate. Serve dusted with sifted pure icing (confectioners') sugar, if you like.

serves 20
prep + cook time 3 hours
(+ standing & cooling)
storage Cake will keep in an airtight container in the refrigerator for up to 3 months. Cut the cake straight from the fridge, then bring to room temperature before serving.

raspberry & almond mascarpone cake

- 500g (1 pound) butter, softened
- 3 cups (660g) caster (superfine) sugar
- 8 eggs
- 2 cups (300g) plain (all-purpose) flour
- 1½ cups (225g) self-raising flour
- 1 cup (125g) ground almonds
- 1 cup (250ml) milk
- 1 cup (140g) toasted slivered almonds, chopped finely
- 400g (12½ ounces) fresh or frozen raspberries
- 400g (12½ ounces) vienna almonds

mascarpone cream
- 750g (1½ pounds) mascarpone cheese
- 300g (9½ ounces) sour cream
- 1 cup (160g) icing (confectioners') sugar
- ⅓ cup (80ml) Cointreau or Grand Marnier

1 Preheat oven to 160°C/325°F. Grease a deep 30cm (12-inch) round cake pan; line base and sides with two layers of baking paper, extending 5cm (2-inches) above edge of pan.

2 Beat butter and sugar in a large bowl with an electric mixer until light and fluffy. Add eggs, one at a time, beating until just combined between additions (the mixture may appear curdled at this stage).

3 Transfer mixture to a very large bowl; fold in sifted flours, ground almonds and milk in three batches. Fold in chopped almonds and raspberries, then spread mixture into prepared pan.

4 Bake cake for 1 hour, then reduce oven temperature to 150°C/300°F and bake a further 1 hour. Stand cake 20 minutes; turn, top-side up, onto a wire rack to cool.

5 Meanwhile make mascarpone cream.

6 Using a large serrated knife, split cake into three layers. Place base layer onto a serving plate; spread with a third of the mascarpone cream, repeat layering, finishing with mascarpone cream. Decorate top of cake with vienna almonds.

mascarpone cream
Beat mascarpone, sour cream and icing sugar in a large bowl with an electric mixer until soft peaks form; stir in liqueur.

serves 25
prep + cook time 2 hours
45 minutes (+ cooling time)
storage Cake (without filling) will
keep in an airtight container for up
to 2 days. Split and fill cake on day of
serving. Cake (without filling) can be
frozen for up to 3 months.

ALMONDS flat, pointy-tipped nuts with a pitted brown shell enclosing a creamy white kernel which is covered by a brown skin.

ground also known as almond meal; nuts powdered to a coarse flour-like texture.

vienna almonds are toffee-coated almonds available from selected supermarkets, nut stands and gourmet food and specialty confectionery stores.

BAKING PAPER also called parchment paper or baking parchment, a silicone-coated paper primarily used for lining baking pans and trays so cakes and biscuits won't stick, making removal easy.

BICARBONATE OF SODA also known as baking or carb soda.

BISCUITS, PLAIN SWEET also known as cookies; a crisp sweet biscuit without icing or filling, we use Nice or Milk Arrowroot varieties.

BUTTER use salted or unsalted (sweet) butter; 125g is equal to one stick (4 ounces) of butter.

BUTTERMILK originally the term given to the slightly sour liquid left after butter was churned from cream, today it is made similarly to yoghurt. Sold alongside all fresh milk products in supermarkets; despite the implication of its name, it is low in fat.

CARAMEL TOP 'N' FILL a caramel filling made from milk and cane sugar. Can be used straight from the can for cheesecakes, slices and tarts. Has similar qualities to sweetened condensed milk, only a thicker, caramel consistency; great to use in caramel desserts.

CHOCOLATE

Choc Bits also known as chocolate chips or chocolate morsels; comes in milk, white and dark chocolate varieties. Contain an emulsifier, so hold their shape in baking and are ideal for decorating.

dark cooking also known as compound chocolate; good for cooking as it doesn't require tempering and sets at room temperature. Made with vegetable fat instead of cocoa butter so it lacks the rich, buttery flavour of eating chocolate. Cocoa butter is the most expensive component in chocolate, so the substitution of a vegetable fat means that compound chocolate is much cheaper to produce.

dark eating made of cocoa liquor, cocoa butter and sugar.

Melts small discs of compound milk, white or dark chocolate ideal for melting and moulding.

milk eating most popular eating chocolate, mild and very sweet; similar in make-up to dark eating chocolate, with the difference being the addition of milk solids.

white contains no cocoa solids but derives its sweet flavour from cocoa butter. Very sensitive to heat.

CINNAMON available both in the piece (called sticks or quills) and ground into powder; one of the world's most common spices, used universally as a sweet, fragrant flavouring for both sweet and savoury foods. The dried inner bark of the shoots of the Sri Lankan native cinnamon tree; much of what is sold as the real thing is in fact cassia, Chinese cinnamon, from the bark of the cassia tree. Cheaper to process than true cinnamon, it is often blended with Sri Lankan cinnamon to produce the type of "cinnamon" most commonly found in supermarkets.

CINNAMON SUGAR a combination of ground cinnamon and caster sugar. To make your own, combine ½ cup caster sugar with 1 teaspoon cinnamon.

COCOA POWDER also known as cocoa; dried, unsweetened, roasted then ground cocoa beans.

COCONUT

desiccated dried, unsweetened, finely shredded coconut flesh.

essence produced from coconut flavouring, oil and alcohol.

flaked dried, flaked coconut.

shredded strips of dried coconut.

COFFEE LIQUEUR we use Kahlúa or Tia Maria, but you can use your favourite brand.

glossary

COINTREAU a citrus-flavoured liqueur based on oranges. Use your favourite brand.

CORNFLOUR also known as cornstarch; used as a thickening agent. Available as 100% maize (corn) and wheaten cornflour.

CREAM CHEESE also known as Philadelphia or Philly, a soft cow's-milk cheese. Also available as spreadable light cream cheese – a blend of cottage and cream cheeses. Sold in supermarkets.

CREAM OF TARTAR the acid ingredient in baking powder; added to confectionery mixtures to help prevent sugar from crystallising. Keeps frostings creamy and improves volume when beating egg whites.

CREAM we use fresh cream, unless otherwise stated.
pouring also known as pure cream; has no additives unlike commercially thickened cream. Minimum fat content 35%.
sour thick commercially-cultured soured cream. Minimum fat content 35%.
thick we used thick cream with 48% fat content.
thickened a whipping cream containing a thickener. Minimum fat content 35%.

CURRANTS, DRIED tiny, almost black raisins, so-named after a grape variety that originated in Corinth, Greece.

CUSTARD POWDER instant mixture used to make pouring custard; similar to North American instant pudding mixes.

DATES fruit of the date palm tree, eaten fresh or dried, on their own or in prepared dishes. About 4cm to 6cm in length, oval and plump, thin-skinned, with a honey-sweet flavour and sticky texture. Best known, perhaps, for their inclusion in sticky toffee pudding; also found in muesli; muffins, scones and cakes; compotes and stewed fruit desserts.

FLOUR
plain an all-purpose flour made from wheat.
self-raising plain flour sifted with baking powder in the proportion of 1 cup flour to 2 teaspoons baking powder.
wholemeal flours milled from the whole wheat grain (bran, germ and flour). Available in both plain and self-raising varieties.

GOLDEN SYRUP a by-product of refined sugarcane; pure maple syrup or honey can be substituted.

HAZELNUTS also known as filberts; plump, grape-sized, rich, sweet nut.
ground also known as hazelnut meal.

HUNDREDS & THOUSANDS also called nonpareils; tiny sugar-syrup-coated sugar crystals that come in bright colours. Used to decorate cakes and other party foods.

JAM also known as preserve or conserve; usually made from fruit.

JELLY CRYSTALS a powdered mixture of gelatine, sweetener, and artificial fruit flavouring that's used to make a moulded, translucent, quivering dessert. Also known as jello.

LEMON BUTTER also known as lemon cheese or lemon spread; a smooth spread, usually made from lemons, butter and eggs.

LOLLIES confectionery; also known as sweets or candy.

MAPLE SYRUP a thin syrup distilled from the sap of the maple tree. Maple-flavoured syrup or pancake syrup is not an adequate substitute for the real thing.

MASCARPONE CHEESE an Italian fresh cultured-cream product made in much the same way as yoghurt. White to creamy yellow in colour, with a buttery-rich, luscious texture. Soft, creamy and spreadable, it is used in many Italian desserts and as an accompaniment to a dessert of fresh fruit.

MARMALADE a preserve, usually based on citrus fruit.

MARSALA a fortified Italian wine produced in the region surrounding the Sicilian city of Marsala; recognisable by its intense amber colour and complex aroma. Often used in cooking, especially in sauces, risottos and desserts.

MILK we use full-cream homogenised milk unless otherwise specified.

evaporated unsweetened canned milk from which water has been extracted by evaporation. Evaporated skim or low-fat milk has 0.3 per cent fat content.

skim sometimes labelled "no-fat"; both have 0.1 per cent fat content.

sweetened condensed a canned milk product consisting of milk with more than half the water content removed and sugar added.

MIXED DRIED FRUIT a mix of sultanas, raisins, currants, mixed peel and cherries.

MIXED PEEL candied citrus peel.

MIXED SPICE a classic mixture generally containing caraway, allspice, coriander, cumin, nutmeg and ginger, although cinnamon and other spices can be added. It is used with fruit and in cakes.

NUTMEG a strong and pungent spice ground from the dried nut of an evergreen tree native to Indonesia. Usually found ground but the flavour is more intense from a whole nut, available from spice shops, so it's best to grate your own. Used most often in baking and milk-based desserts, but also works nicely in savoury dishes. Found in mixed spice blends.

NUTS, HOW TO ROAST place shelled, peeled nuts, in a single layer, on an oven tray, roast in a moderate oven 8-10 minutes. Take care to avoid burning nuts.

POPPY SEEDS tiny black seeds with a pungent flavour; store in an airtight container in a cool place or in the freezer.

RAISINS dried sweet grapes.

RHUBARB only eat its thick, celery-like stalks, as the leaves contain a toxic substance.

SEMOLINA made from durum wheat; milled into either fine or coarse granules.

SUGAR

brown soft, finely granulated sugar retaining molasses for its characteristic colour and flavour.

caster also known as superfine or finely granulated table sugar.

demerara a rich, golden-coloured small-grained crystal sugar with a subtle molasses flavour.

icing sugar also known as confectioners' sugar or powdered sugar; granulated sugar crushed together with a small amount of added cornflour.

raw natural light-brown coloured granulated sugar with a honey-like taste.

white a coarse, granulated table sugar, also known as crystal sugar.

SULTANAS dried grapes, also known as golden raisins.

SWEET SHERRY fortified wine.

TANGELO an orange-coloured loose-skinned, juicy, sweetly-tart citrus fruit with few seeds.

TREACLE thick, dark syrup not unlike molasses; a by-product of sugar refining.

VANILLA

bean dried long, thin pod from a tropical golden orchid; the minuscule black seeds inside the bean are used to impart a luscious vanilla flavour in baking and desserts. A whole bean can be placed in the sugar container to make the vanilla sugar that's often called for in recipes.

extract made by pulping chopped vanilla beans with a mixture of alcohol and water. This gives a very strong solution, and only a couple of drops are needed to flavour most dishes.

paste made from vanilla pods and contains real seeds. It is highly concentrated and 1 teaspoon replaces a whole vanilla pod without mess or fuss as you neither have to split or scrape the pod. It is found in the baking aisle of many supermarkets.

YEAST a 7g (¼ oz) sachet of dried yeast (2 teaspoons) is equal to 15g (½ oz) compressed yeast, if substituting one for the other.

YOGHURT we used plain, unflavoured yoghurt, unless otherwise specified.

greek-style full-cream yoghurt, often made from sheep's milk; its thick, smooth consistency, almost like whipped cream, is attained by draining off the milk liquids.

conversion chart

measures

One Australian metric measuring cup holds approximately 250ml, one Australian metric tablespoon holds 20ml, one Australian metric teaspoon holds 5ml. The difference between one country's measuring cups and another's is within a 2- or 3-teaspoon variance, and will not affect your cooking results. North America, New Zealand and the United Kingdom use a 15ml tablespoon. All cup and spoon measurements are level. The most accurate way of measuring dry ingredients is to weigh them. When measuring liquids, use a clear glass or plastic jug with metric markings. We use large eggs with an average weight of 60g.

dry measures

METRIC	IMPERIAL
15g	½oz
30g	1oz
60g	2oz
90g	3oz
125g	4oz (¼lb)
155g	5oz
185g	6oz
220g	7oz
250g	8oz (½lb)
280g	9oz
315g	10oz
345g	11oz
375g	12oz (¾lb)
410g	13oz
440g	14oz
470g	15oz
500g	16oz (1lb)
750g	24oz (1½lb)
1kg	32oz (2lb)

liquid measures

METRIC	IMPERIAL
30ml	1 fluid oz
60ml	2 fluid oz
100ml	3 fluid oz
125ml	4 fluid oz
150ml	5 fluid oz
190ml	6 fluid oz
250ml	8 fluid oz
300ml	10 fluid oz
500ml	16 fluid oz
600ml	20 fluid oz
1000ml (1 litre)	1¾ pints

length measures

METRIC	IMPERIAL
3mm	⅛in
6mm	¼in
1cm	½in
2cm	¾in
2.5cm	1in
5cm	2in
6cm	2½in
8cm	3in
10cm	4in
13cm	5in
15cm	6in
18cm	7in
20cm	8in
23cm	9in
25cm	10in
28cm	11in
30cm	12in (1ft)

oven temperatures

These oven temperatures are only a guide for conventional ovens. For fan-forced ovens, check the manufacturer's manual.

	°C (CELSIUS)	°F (FAHRENHEIT)
Very slow	120	250
Slow	150	275-300
Moderately slow	160	325
Moderate	180	350-375
Moderately hot	200	400
Hot	220	425-450
Very hot	240	475

The imperial measurements used in these recipes are approximate only. Measurements for cake pans are approximate only. Using same-shaped cake pans of a similar size should not affect the outcome of your baking. We measure the inside top of the cake pan to determine sizes.

A

angel food cake 55

B

banana caramel layer cake 26
black forest mud cake 30
brandied buttercream 38
brandy
  brandied buttercream 38
  brandy marmalade
    chocolate cake 11
  brandy syrup 11
brandy marmalade
  chocolate cake 11
buttercream
  brandied 38
  chocolate 48

C

candied citrus 60
candied citrus cake 60
caramel angel food cake
  with sugared pecans 43
caramel cream
  cheese frosting 43
celebration cakes
  candied citrus cake 60
  gluten-free dairy-free spicy
    fruit cake 71
  lemon curd meringue cake
    with blueberries 68
  raspberry & almond
    marscapone cake 72
  rich chocolate fruit cake 67
  whiskey fruit cake 63
chocolate & strawberry
  meringue gateau 64
chocolate buttercream 48
chocolate cake
  black forest mud cake 30
  brandy marmalade
    chocolate cake 11

chocolate and strawberry
  meringue gateau 64
chocolate chiffon cake 38
chocolate, prune & almond
  fudge cake 7
date & chocolate torte 15
flourless chocolate cake with
  mint toffee ice-cream 12
gluten-free chocolate cake 20
hazelnut mud cake with
  fudge frosting 19
rich chocolate cake with
  strawberries & ganache 8
rich chocolate fruit cake 67
sacher torte 16
chocolate chiffon cake 38
chocolate ganache 8
chocolate icing 16, 51
chocolate, prune & almond
  fudge cake 7
cinnamon cream 51
cream cheese lemon cake 56
custard filling 37

D

dark chocolate
  ganache 11, 30
date & chocolate torte 15
devil's food cake 44

F

feather-light cakes
  angel food cake 55
  caramel angel food cake
    with sugared pecans 43
  cream cheese
    lemon cake 56
  devil's food cake 44
  honey spice
    sponge cake 52
  marbled victoria sponge 48
  mocha spice sponge cake 51
  raspberry chiffon cake 46

index

frosting
 caramel cream cheese 43
 fudge 19
 marscapone 33
 rich chocolate 44
fruit cake
 gluten-free dairy-free spicy 71
 rich chocolate 67
 whiskey 63
fudge frosting 19

G
ganache 67
 chocolate 8
 dark chocolate 11, 30
glacé icing 60
gluten-free
 chocolate cake 20
 spicy fruit cake 71

H
hazelnut mud cake with
 fudge frosting 19
honey spice sponge cake 52

I
icing
 chocolate 16, 51
 glacé 60
 raspberry 47

L
layered cakes
 banana caramel
  layer cake 26
 lemon yoghurt cake with
  lemon curd frosting 25
 mango, coconut &
  marscapone sponge 29
 pink velvet cake 33
 tiramisu torte 34
 torta di mamma 37

lemon curd 25, 68
lemon curd meringue cake
 with blueberries 68
lemon yoghurt cake with lemon
 curd frosting 25

M
mango, coconut &
 marscapone sponge 29
marbled victoria sponge 48
marscapone
 cream 72
 filling 29
 frosting 33
mocha spice sponge cake 51

P
pink velvet cake 33

R
raspberry
 icing 47
 raspberry & almond
  marscapone cake 72
 raspberry chiffon cake 46
raspberry & almond
 marscapone cake 72
raspberry chiffon cake 46
raspberry icing 47
rich chocolate cake with
 strawberries & ganache 8
rich chocolate
 frosting 44
rich chocolate fruit cake 67

S
sacher torte 16
sponge cake
 mango, coconut &
  marscapone 29
 marbled victoria 48
 mocha spice 51

strawberries
 rich chocolate cake with
  strawberries & ganache 8
syrup, brandy 11

T
tiramisu torte 34
toffee 12
torta di mamma 37
torte
 date & chocolate 15
 sacher 16
 tiramisu 34
 torta di mamma 37

W
walnut praline 37
whiskey fruit cake 63

Published in 2013 by Bauer Media Books, Sydney
Bauer Media Books are published by Bauer Media Limited
54 Park St, Sydney
GPO Box 4088, Sydney, NSW 2001.
phone (02) 9282 8618; fax (02) 9126 3702
www.awwcookbooks.com.au

MEDIA GROUP

BAUER MEDIA BOOKS
Publishing Director - Gerry Reynolds
Publisher - Sally Wright
Director of Sales, Marketing & Rights - Brian Cearnes
Editorial & Food Director - Pamela Clark
Creative Director - Hieu Chi Nguyen
Food Concept Director - Sophia Young

Published and Distributed in the United Kingdom by Octopus Publishing Group
Endeavour House
189 Shaftesbury Avenue
London WC2H 8JY
United Kingdom
phone (+44)(0)207 632 5400; fax (+44)(0)207 632 5405
info@octopus-publishing.co.uk;
www.octopusbooks.co.uk

Printed by Toppan Printing Co., China

International foreign language rights, Brian Cearnes, Bauer Media Books
bcearnes@bauer-media.com.au

A catalogue record for this book is available from the British Library.
ISBN 978-1-74245-355-2
© Bauer Media Limited 2013
ABN 18 053 273 546